NATURAL WONDERS
VICTORIA FALLS

by Katie Chanez

Ideas for Parents and Teachers

Pogo Books let children practice reading informational text while introducing them to nonfiction features such as headings, labels, sidebars, maps, and diagrams, as well as a table of contents, glossary, and index.

Carefully leveled text with a strong photo match offers early fluent readers the support they need to succeed.

Before Reading

- "Walk" through the book and point out the various nonfiction features. Ask the student what purpose each feature serves.
- Look at the glossary together. Read and discuss the words.

Read the Book

- Have the child read the book independently.
- Invite them to list questions that arise from reading.

After Reading

- Discuss the child's questions. Talk about how they might find answers to those questions.
- Prompt the child to think more. Ask: Did you know about Victoria Falls before reading this book? What more would you like to learn about the falls?

Pogo Books are published by Jump!
5357 Penn Avenue South
Minneapolis, MN 55419
www.jumplibrary.com

Copyright © 2025 Jump!
International copyright reserved in all countries. No part of this book may be reproduced in any form without written permission from the publisher.

Library of Congress Cataloging-in-Publication Data

Names: Chanez, Katie, author.
Title: Victoria falls / by Katie Chanez.
Description: Minneapolis : Jump!, Inc., 2025.
Series: Natural wonders | Includes index.
Audience: Ages 7-10
Identifiers: LCCN 2024037223 (print)
LCCN 2024037224 (ebook)
ISBN 9798892135498 (hardcover)
ISBN 9798892135504 (paperback)
ISBN 9798892135511 (ebook)
Subjects: LCSH: Waterfalls–Juvenile fiction.
Victoria Falls (Zambia and Zimbabwe) –Juvenile fiction.
Zimbabwe–Juvenile fiction. | Zambia–Juvenile fiction.
Classification: LCC DT3140.V54 C43 2025 (print)
LCC DT3140.V54 (ebook)
DDC 968.91–dc23/eng/20241029
LC record available at https://lccn.loc.gov/2024037223
LC ebook record available at https://lccn.loc.gov/2024037224

Editor: Alyssa Sorenson
Designer: Molly Ballanger

Photo Credits: Jixin YU/Shutterstock, cover; Stephan Roeger/Shutterstock, 1; THP Creative/iStock, 3; Klara Bakalarova/Dreamstime, 4; Tahseenamjad/Shutterstock, 5; bayazed/Shutterstock, 6-7; Shab42/Shutterstock, 8; RuqayaMai/Shutterstock, 9 (top); Marc Bode/Shutterstock, 9 (bottom); InnaFelker/iStock, 10-11; guenterguni/iStock, 12-13; ichywong/Shutterstock, 14-15; Norbert Eisele-Hein/imageBROKER/SuperStock, 16; nini/iStock, 17; APATOW PROD./COLUMBIA PICT./GH THREE/NOMINATED FIL/Roger de la Harpe/SuperStock, 18-19; fotoguy22/iStock, 20-21; VILTVART/Shutterstock, 23.

Printed in the United States of America at Corporate Graphics in North Mankato, Minnesota.

TABLE OF CONTENTS

CHAPTER 1
Falling Water...4

CHAPTER 2
How the Falls Formed.....................................8

CHAPTER 3
The Falls Today..16

QUICK FACTS & TOOLS
At a Glance..22
Glossary..23
Index..24
To Learn More...24

CHAPTER 1
FALLING WATER

The Zambezi River flows in Africa. Along the border of Zambia and Zimbabwe, it drops! It falls nearly 355 feet (108 meters).

Zambezi River

It drops into Batoka **Gorge**, creating Victoria Falls. Victoria Falls is the largest falling sheet of water in the world. It is nearly 5,600 feet (1,700 m) long!

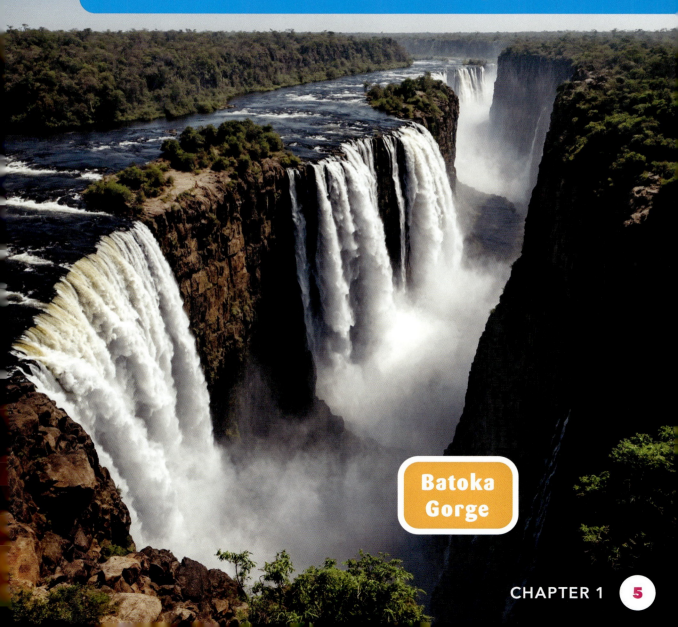

Batoka Gorge

CHAPTER 1 5

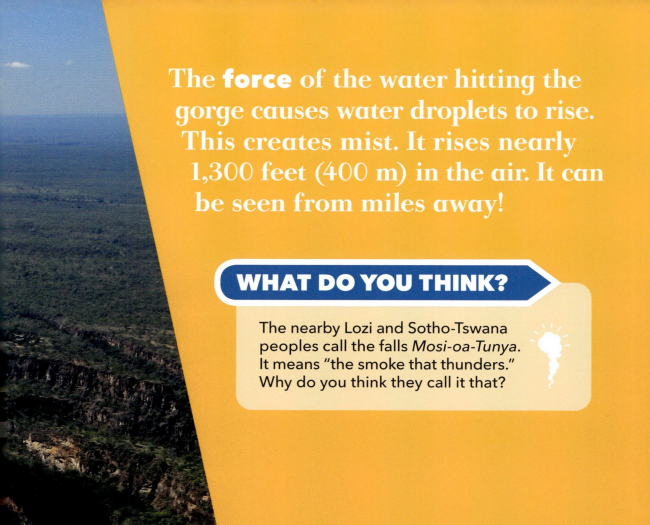

The **force** of the water hitting the gorge causes water droplets to rise. This creates mist. It rises nearly 1,300 feet (400 m) in the air. It can be seen from miles away!

WHAT DO YOU THINK?

The nearby Lozi and Sotho-Tswana peoples call the falls *Mosi-oa-Tunya*. It means "the smoke that thunders." Why do you think they call it that?

CHAPTER 1

CHAPTER 2
HOW THE FALLS FORMED

The falls started forming millions of years ago. Volcanoes **erupted**. They covered the area in **lava**. The lava cooled. It formed a **plateau** made of basalt rock. The basalt cooled more. It cracked.

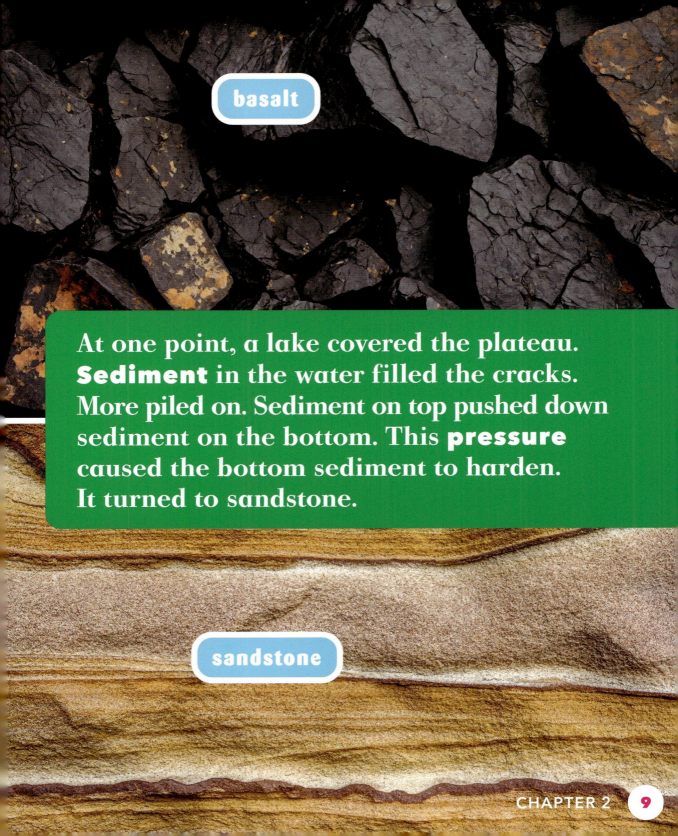

basalt

At one point, a lake covered the plateau. **Sediment** in the water filled the cracks. More piled on. Sediment on top pushed down sediment on the bottom. This **pressure** caused the bottom sediment to harden. It turned to sandstone.

sandstone

Earth is made of **tectonic plates**. They shift and lift. The plates lifted the plateau. The Zambezi River began to flow over the plateau. It began to **erode** the sandstone.

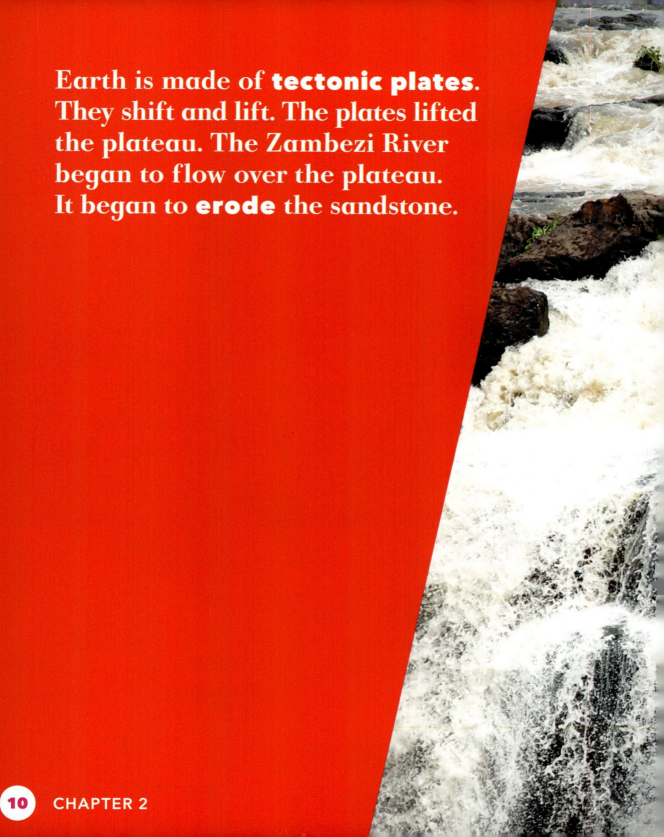

CHAPTER 2

Sandstone is softer than basalt. It erodes much faster. This created Batoka Gorge. The falls as we see them formed 250,000 to 100,000 years ago! At the bottom, water still erodes the sandstone.

TAKE A LOOK!

How did Victoria Falls form? Take a look!

1. Volcanoes erupted. Lava cooled.

2. A plateau of basalt formed. It cracked.
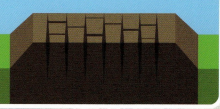

3. Water covered it. Sediment filled the cracks and turned to sandstone.
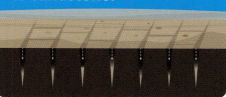

4. Tectonic plates moved. River water eroded the sandstone and formed the gorge and falls.

CHAPTER 2

Victoria Falls is known for its rainbows. The falling water creates a lot of mist. When sunlight shines through the mist, rainbows form!

DID YOU KNOW?

Lunar rainbows also appear here. These form from moonlight. They are hard to see.

CHAPTER 2

CHAPTER 3
THE FALLS TODAY

People have lived by the falls for 3 million years! Scientists have found **traces** of people from the **Stone Age**. People still live in nearby towns. They share their **cultures** with visitors.

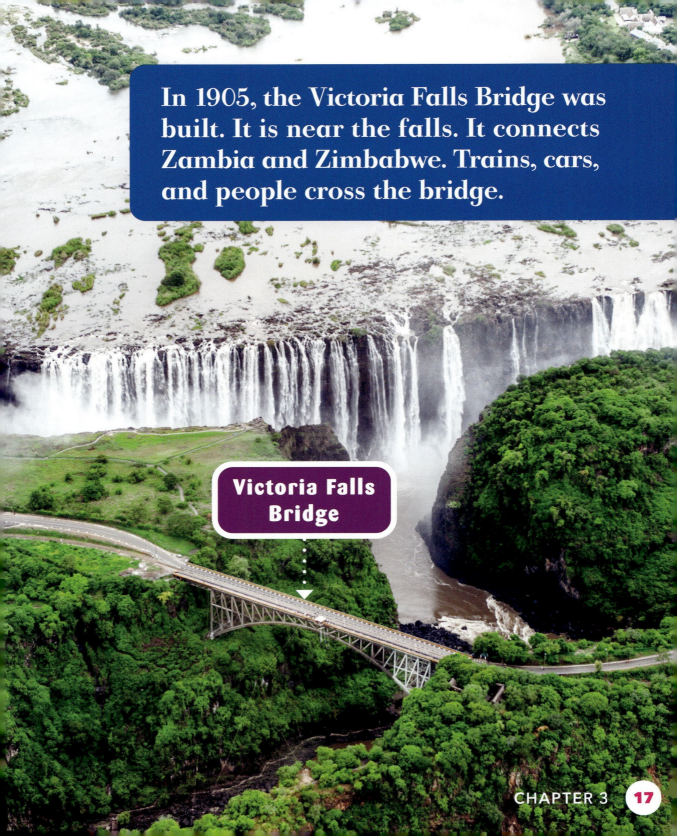

In 1905, the Victoria Falls Bridge was built. It is near the falls. It connects Zambia and Zimbabwe. Trains, cars, and people cross the bridge.

Victoria Falls Bridge

CHAPTER 3 17

There are many things to do here. **National parks** are on each side of the river. Visitors boat on the Zambezi River. There are paths to walk on. Some people bungee jump or zip line!

WHAT DO YOU THINK?

Many people travel to see the falls. Would you like to visit? What would you like to do or see here?

CHAPTER 3

The falls are always changing. **Climate change** affects how much rain falls here. The more rain, the more water flows over the falls. The opposite is also true. In 2019, the falls nearly ran dry. By protecting Earth, we can protect the falls for all to enjoy!

CHAPTER 3   21

QUICK FACTS & TOOLS

AT A GLANCE

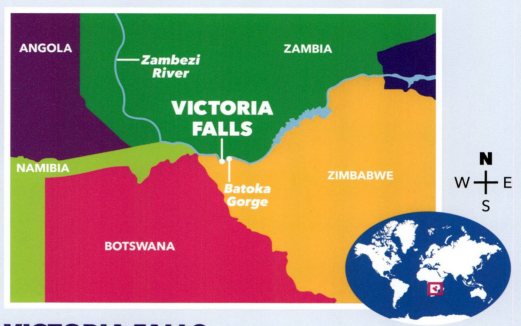

VICTORIA FALLS

Location: border of Zambia and Zimbabwe in Africa

Date Formed: about 250,000 to 100,000 years ago

How They Formed: water eroded sandstone

Number of Yearly Visitors: more than 1 million people

GLOSSARY

climate change: Changes in weather and weather patterns that happen because of human activity.

cultures: The ideas, customs, traditions, and ways of life of groups of people.

erode: To wear away with water, wind, heat, or ice.

erupted: Threw out lava, hot ash, and steam.

force: Strength or power.

gorge: A deep valley or ravine.

lava: Hot, liquid rock that comes out of the earth.

lunar: Of or having to do with the Moon.

national parks: Areas controlled by governments to preserve special places in nature.

plateau: A broad, flat area of high land.

pressure: The force produced by pressing on something.

sediment: Minerals, mud, gravel, or sand, or a combination of these, that have been carried to a place by water, wind, or glaciers.

Stone Age: A period in history when stone was used to make tools and weapons.

tectonic plates: Large, flat sheets of rock that make up Earth's crust.

traces: Small, visible signs something has happened or someone has been somewhere.

QUICK FACTS & TOOLS

INDEX

basalt 8, 12, 13
Batoka Gorge 5, 7, 12, 13
climate change 21
cultures 16
erode 10, 12, 13
lava 8, 13
mist 7, 14
Mosi-oa-Tunya 7
national parks 18
plateau 8, 9, 10, 13
pressure 9
rainbows 14
sandstone 9, 10, 12, 13
sediment 9, 13
Stone Age 16
tectonic plates 10, 13
Victoria Falls Bridge 17
visitors 16, 18
volcanoes 8, 13
Zambezi River 4, 10, 13, 18
Zambia 4, 17
Zimbabwe 4, 17

TO LEARN MORE

Finding more information is as easy as 1, 2, 3.

1. Go to www.factsurfer.com
2. Enter "VictoriaFalls" into the search box.
3. Choose your book to see a list of websites.